All Roads Lead to Rome

Written by Claire Owen

Italy

My name is Tomasso. I live in the Abruzzo region of Italy. What do you think life was like during the Roman Empire? How do you think the ancient Romans used mathematics?

Contents

Wherever you see me, you'll find activities to try and questions to answer.

The Roman Empire

The Roman Empire was one of the largest and most powerful civilizations in the history of the world. It began about 2,000 years ago and lasted for more than 500 years. At its peak, Rome ruled over more than 50 million people—about one-fifth of the world's population at the time. The empire covered an area of some 2.5 million square miles—about twice the size of Mexico.

The people of the Roman Empire spoke many languages and had different ways of life and different religions. Under Roman rule, however, they followed the same systems of law and government.

Britain

Ancient Europe

Rome

Africa

Ancient Egypt

civilization a highly developed and organized society with written language, arts, sciences, and government

Rome has been an important center for so long that it is sometimes called the Eternal City. This painting of the walled city was made in the early 1400s.

According to legend, the city of Rome was founded by Romulus and Remus, the twin grandsons of a king. As babies, the twins were thrown into a river by their wicked uncle. Washed ashore, Romulus and Remus were nursed by a wolf until a shepherd found them.

Estimate the total population of the world at the peak of the Roman Empire.

The Colosseum

There were many splendid buildings in ancient
Rome. One of the most famous is the Colosseum.
Completed in the year 80, this huge amphitheater
had four levels and could seat 50,000 people.
The Colosseum had 80 exits, called *vomitoria*.
It is claimed that all of the people in the audience
could make their way out of the Colosseum
in just 5 minutes!

Each year, thousands of
people visit the ruins of
the Colosseum.

amphitheater   a round or oval building that has rows of seats
gradually rising around an open space

About how many people would leave the Colosseum by each exit? How many people would have to leave by each exit, per second, in order to clear a full Colosseum in 5 minutes?

Colosseum Facts

- The wooden floor of the Colosseum was covered in sand. The Latin word for sand is *arena*.

- Beneath the floor of the Colosseum was a complex system of corridors, ramps, cages for wild animals, and mechanical elevators.

- In the early days, probably before the underground corridors were dug, the Colosseum could be flooded with water for mock naval battles!

- Spectators were protected from the hot sun by a huge awning made up of "sails."

complex   made up of different parts; not simple

Roman Soldiers

The Roman Empire was so large and so widespread
that a huge army was needed to defend its borders.
The Roman army was divided into sections called
legions, and each legion was made up of thousands
of soldiers. At times, as many as 300,000 soldiers
might have served in the Roman army.

A Roman Legion

How many regular Roman soldiers would you expect there to be in a century? Why? In fact, how many soldiers were there in a century?

- Regular soldiers lived and worked in small tent groups of 8 men.

- A century was made up of 10 tent groups, led by a centurion.

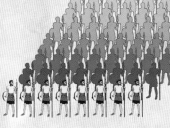

- A regular cohort was made up of 6 centuries.

How many regular soldiers were there in a regular cohort? ... a special cohort? ... a legion? How many centurions commanded a legion?

- A special cohort was made up of only 5 centuries, but each century had double the usual number of soldiers.

- A Roman legion consisted of 9 regular cohorts and one special cohort.

Roman Roads

The ancient Romans built a vast network of paved roads throughout their empire. The total length of the roads is thought to be more than 50,000 miles—about twice the distance around the equator! Roman roads followed the most direct route between two places. Where necessary, bridges and tunnels were built so that the roads could be straight and level.

The Appian Way (left) is a famous road built by the Romans. It was so well made that it is still used today. Many modern roads in Europe follow old Roman routes.

Did You Know?

The Romans had a kind of "pony express." It was possible to send a letter to Rome from as far away as Gaul (modern-day France) in just a few days.

pony express   a system of riders on very fast ponies that was once used to carry mail in the western U.S.

It cost about 10,000 *sesterces* to build each mile of road. (A sesterce was a bronze coin.)

A regular soldier earned about 900 sesterces a year. How many miles of road could be built for the same cost as the annual wages of a century of soldiers?

Measuring a Mile

To measure distances, the Romans counted the paces taken by soldiers marching at a steady rate. One pace was two steps: left, right. A marker stone was placed every *mille passus*, or thousand paces, along a Roman road. The word *mile* comes from *mille*, and today the markers are called *milestones*. A Roman mile was about nine-tenths of the length of a modern mile.

The *pes* was a Roman unit of length based on the human foot. Each *passus* was equivalent to 5 pes. Another unit was the *stadium*. A Roman mile was divided into 8 *stadia*.

Roman milestone, Valpusteria, Italy

How many Roman feet were equivalent to one Roman mile? How many Roman miles were equivalent to 1,000 stadia?

Roman Numerals

The distances on milestones were shown with Roman numerals. No one is really certain how these numerals came to be. Some people think that they came from notches on a tally stick. Other people think that some numerals represented hand signs.

Some of the Roman numerals that we write today were not always used in ancient Rome. The number nine, for example, was often written as VIIII rather than IX.

Roman numerals can often be seen on old buildings.

PAVLVS QVINTVS PONTIFEX MAXIMVS
AQVAM IN AGRO BRACCIANENSI
SALVBERRIMIS E FONTIBVS COLLECTAM
VETERIBVS AQVAE ALSIETINAE DVCTIBVS RESTITVTIS
NOVISQVE ADDITIS
XXXV AB MILLIARIO DVXIT

tally stick   a piece of wood with notches marked on it to keep count

Did You Know?

The four on a clock face is usually shown as IIII rather than IV.

Figure It Out

How would you solve these problems?

1. What numbers are shown by these Roman numerals?

   a. VIII   d. XVI

   b. XXXIV   e. LXX

   c. CCLIII   f. MDCLXI

2. Write these numbers as Roman numerals.

   a. 7   d. 13

   b. 26   e. 80

   c. 352

3. Where do you see Roman numerals today?

I = one   C = one hundred
V = five   D = five hundred
X = ten   M = one thousand
L = fifty

I	II	III	IV	V	VI	VII	VIII	IX	X	XI
1	2	3	4	5	6	7	8	9	10	11	12

A Roman Abacus

The Romans used an abacus to help them add, subtract, and perform other calculations with numbers. Some abacuses were made of stone or metal. However, an inexpensive abacus could be made simply by arranging pebbles in grooves in the dirt. The pebbles were called *calculi*. This is the origin of the word *calculate*.

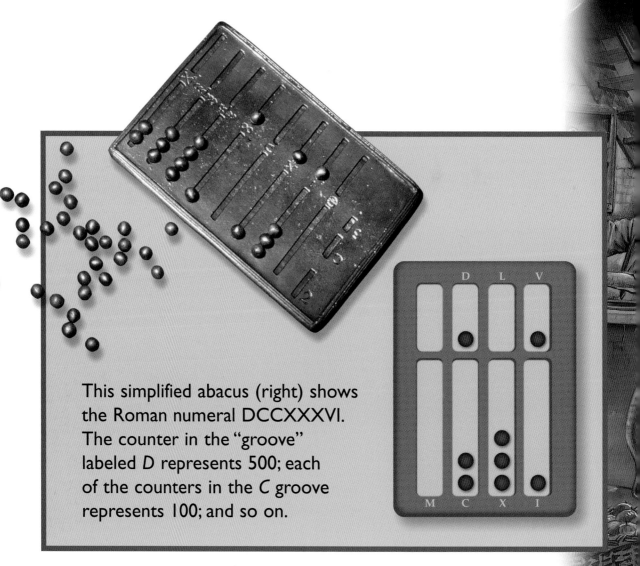

This simplified abacus (right) shows the Roman numeral DCCXXXVI. The counter in the "groove" labeled *D* represents 500; each of the counters in the *C* groove represents 100; and so on.

Add with an Abacus

You will need counters and a copy of the Roman Abacus Blackline Master. Follow these steps to add DCCXVIII and CCCXXXIII. Then create your own addition or subtraction examples.

1. Use counters to show DCCXVIII. Then use more counters (see the dotted outlines below) to add CCCXXXIII.

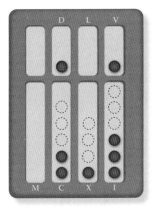

2. Are there more than 4 counters in the *I* groove? If so, replace 5 counters with one counter in the *V* groove.

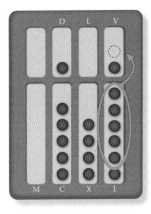

3. Is there more than one counter in the *V* groove? If so, replace 2 counters with one counter in the *X* groove.

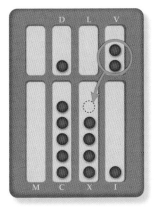

4. Use similar steps to check the *X* groove and the *L* groove, and so on. How could you check that the total is correct?

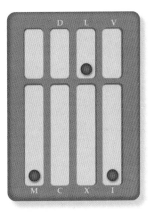

Measuring Up

Using the network of Roman roads, farmers could transport their produce to nearby towns or to ports that shipped goods to faraway places. In Rome itself, the public market was a very busy place. Elected officials called *aediles* supervised the market. One of their most important jobs was to make sure that the traders used standard weights and measures.

The picture above shows tables of standard measures in a Roman marketplace. The "basins" were probably used to measure dry goods such as grain.

In Rome, the foot, or *pes*, was the basic unit of length. This mosaic shows a woman holding a pes measure. The pes was divided into 12 equal parts called *unciae* (oons EE ay).

In how many different ways could 12 unciae be divided into equal parts? When making equal parts, why is 12 a more useful number than 10?

Tipping the Scales

In Rome, a standard one-pes measure weighed one *libra*, that is, one Roman pound. (The word *pound* comes from *libra pondo*, which means "a pound of weight.") Like the pes, the libra was divided into 12 unciae. The words *inch* and *ounce* both come from *unciae*. Today, a pound has 16 ounces, but this did not become standard in England until about the year 1330.

Metal weights were hung on scales like those shown in the carving above.

Weighty Facts

- The abbreviation *lb.* for *pound* comes from the word *libra*.

- The word *libra* also means *balance* or *scales*. Today, the zodiac sign Libra is represented by a pair of balancing scales.

- Today, gold is still measured in 12-ounce pounds called *troy pounds*.

Figure out how many unciae were in each of the fractions of a libra (below). Then write the English fraction names in order, from least to greatest.

The Romans had names for fractions of a pes or libra.

Name	Fraction
bes	two-thirds
deunx	eleven-twelfths
dextans	five-sixths
dodrans	three-fourths
quadrans	one-fourth
quincunx	five-twelfths
semis	one-half
septunx	seven-twelfths
sextans	one-sixth
triens	one-third
uncia	one-twelfth

The End of an Empire

The Roman Empire grew so big that it became expensive to govern and difficult to defend. The empire ended in the year 476, but the influence of the ancient Romans continues to the present day. Many words in the English language come from Latin. Many things that form part of everyday life were introduced or improved by the Romans. For example, the calendar that we use today was invented long ago in ancient Rome.

Over the centuries, the Roman calendar was changed several times to make it more accurate. Two months were added at the beginning of the year. Two other months were renamed after the Roman rulers Julius Caesar and Augustus (right).

The first Roman calendar had only 10 months. Some months were named after Roman gods. Other names came from Latin words for numbers:

5	*quinque*	8	*octo*
6	*sex*	9	*novem*
7	*septem*	10	*decem*

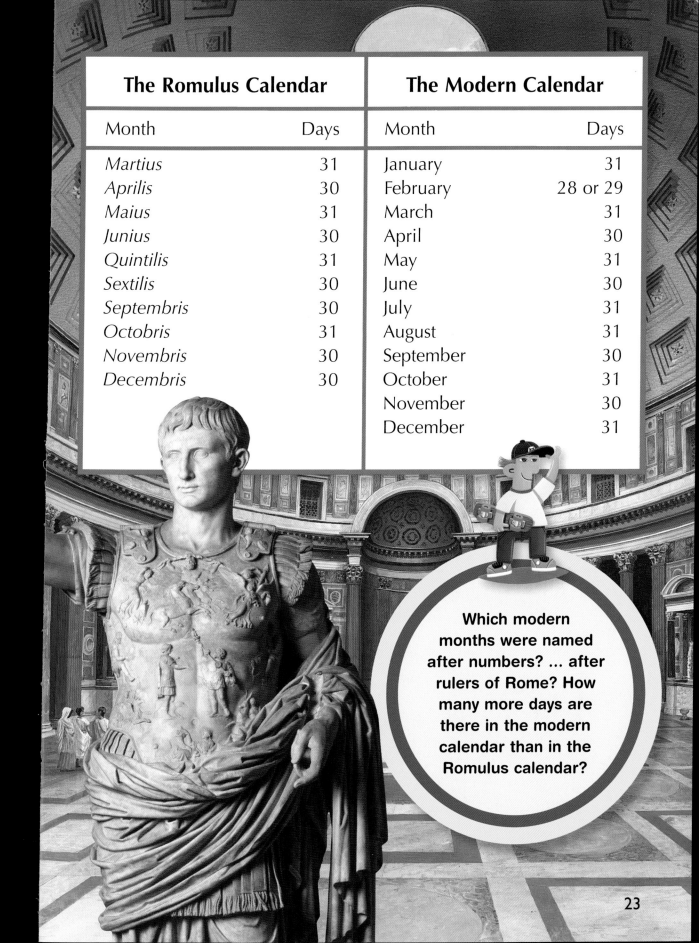

The Romulus Calendar		The Modern Calendar	
Month	Days	Month	Days
Martius	31	January	31
Aprilis	30	February	28 or 29
Maius	31	March	31
Junius	30	April	30
Quintilis	31	May	31
Sextilis	30	June	30
Septembris	30	July	31
Octobris	31	August	31
Novembris	30	September	30
Decembris	30	October	31
		November	30
		December	31

Which modern months were named after numbers? ... after rulers of Rome? How many more days are there in the modern calendar than in the Romulus calendar?

23

Sample Answers

Find out more about Roman weights and measures. For example, you could investigate the Roman units for measuring liquids, such as oil or wine, and dry goods, such as grain.

Page 5   about 250 million

Page 7   625 people per doorway; about
2 people per second

Page 9   100, because *century* means
"100 years"; 80 soldiers in a century;
regular cohort: 480 soldiers
special cohort: 800 soldiers
legion: 5,120 soldiers, 59 centurions

Page 11   about 7 miles

Page 13   5,000 Roman feet; 125 Roman miles

Page 15   1. a. 8   b. 34   c. 253   d. 16   e. 70
     f. 1,661

         2. a. VII   b. XXVI   c. CCCLII
     d. XIII   e. LXXX

Page 19   12: 2 groups of 6; 3 groups of 4;
4 groups of 3; 6 groups of 2

Page 21   8, 11, 10, 9, 3, 5, 6, 7, 2, 4, 1;
one-twelfth, one-sixth, … eleven-twelfths

Page 23   September through December; July and August;
61 more days (62 in a leap year)

Index